Dedicated to the Sadlons, Hotovys and Schlickmans.

You will always have a place at our campfire.

Francis Creek Fjords Coloring Books: Color Your Way Into Western Riding
ISBN-13: 978-0-9971624-0-0

Patti Jo Walter and her husband, Dave Walter, started Francis Creek Fjords (FCF) in 1995. FCF was a Fjord hub for nearly two decades, having Fjords come from all over the United States to be trained, sold on consignment, or bred to their stallion, Fair Acres Ole. Patti Jo began giving riding lessons in 1998, teaching myriad disciplines: huntseat, dressage, jumping, and driving. Today, she continues to instruct dressage and jumping, sharing her passion with anyone wishing to learn and have fun with horses.

Inspired by Patti Jo Walter

Illustrated by Pat Holland

Patricia Holland, born and raised in Northeastern Pennsylvania, attended York Academy of Art to pursue a career in commercial art. Dovetailing her lifelong passions of art and horses, she became a professional horse trainer, illustrating what she saw, what she learned, and the people she met along the way. With humor and wit she juggles these contrasting careers, creating a rich and fulfilling life. She resides and illustrates in Galena, Illinois.

Norwegian Fjord Horses (N.F.H.), featured in many of these drawings, are an offshoot horse breed well known for their gentle disposition, calm demeanor, and great versatility, but it's their loving and humorous personalities that draw in most owners. Mutual affection for these charismatic animals caused Pat and Patti's lives to intersect. Once united, Pat's humor and wit served as the perfect complement to Patti's love of life, forging a lifelong friendship in and out of the pasture, much like the horses they admire.

Pat and Patti created this coloring book series as a fun way of learning horseback riding terminology and concepts for Francis Creek Fjords' students. Pat's skillfully drawn illustrations—filled with humor, life, and laughter—combined with Patti's impressive understanding of horses and students resulted in a colorful array of barnyard characters teaching valuable horse-related lessons you can color.

How to use this book

Step 1: Grab your crayons or colored pencils! (Markers are not recommended)

Step 2: Choose your favorite picture!

Step 3: Color!

Step 4: Have fun!

Don't forget to read the notes and study the images. There are lessons to be learned within these pages.

A Comparison of Western and English Horseback Riding

Both Western and English riders should sit tall and straight in the saddle, with arms relaxed yet tight to their body, and legs hanging naturally along the horse's side.

Western Rider

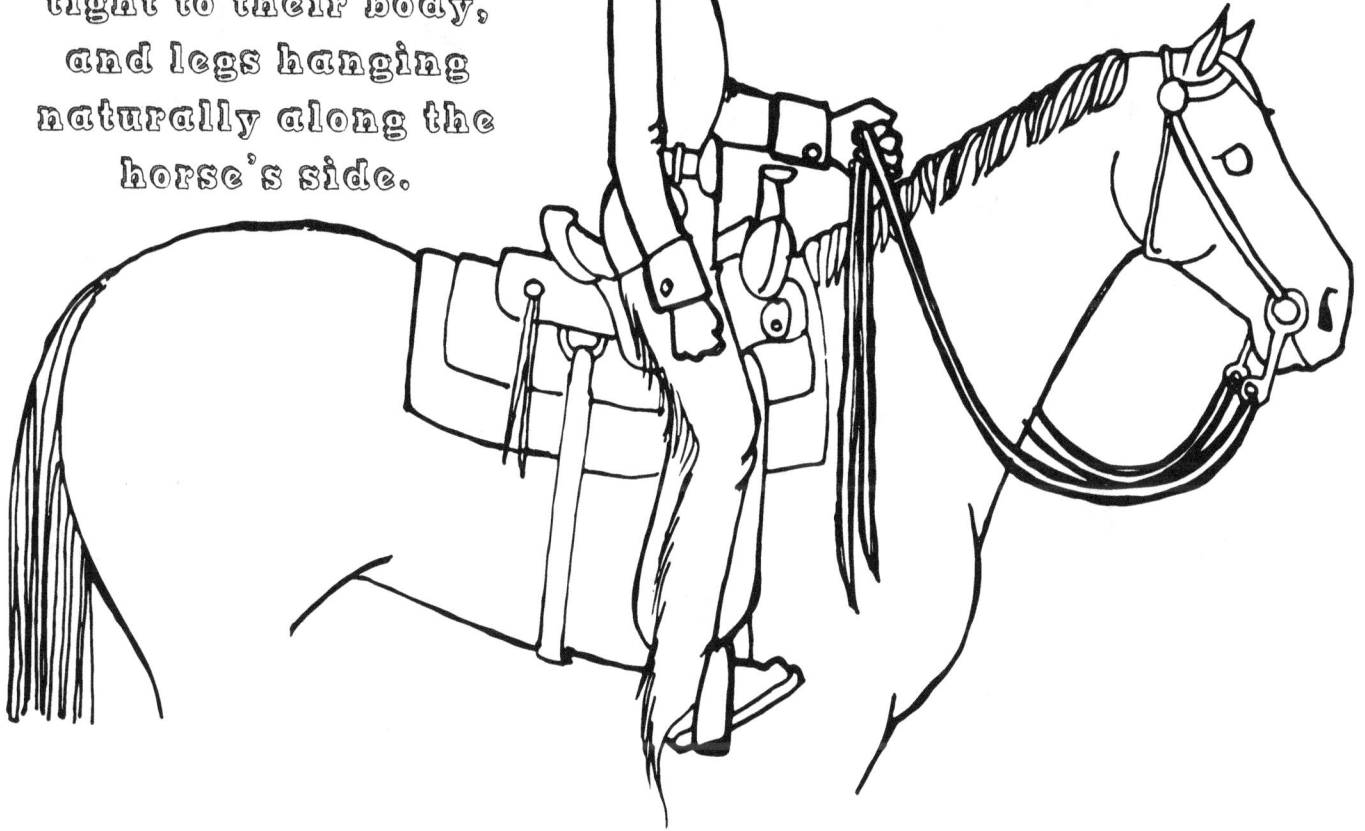

English Rider

Horn

Gullet

Cantle

Roll

Ladigo Holder

Seat

Saddle Strings

Front Rigging Dee

Latigo

Fender

Flank Billet

Skirt

Hobble Strap

Stirrup Leather

Flank Cinch

Stirrup

Front Cinch

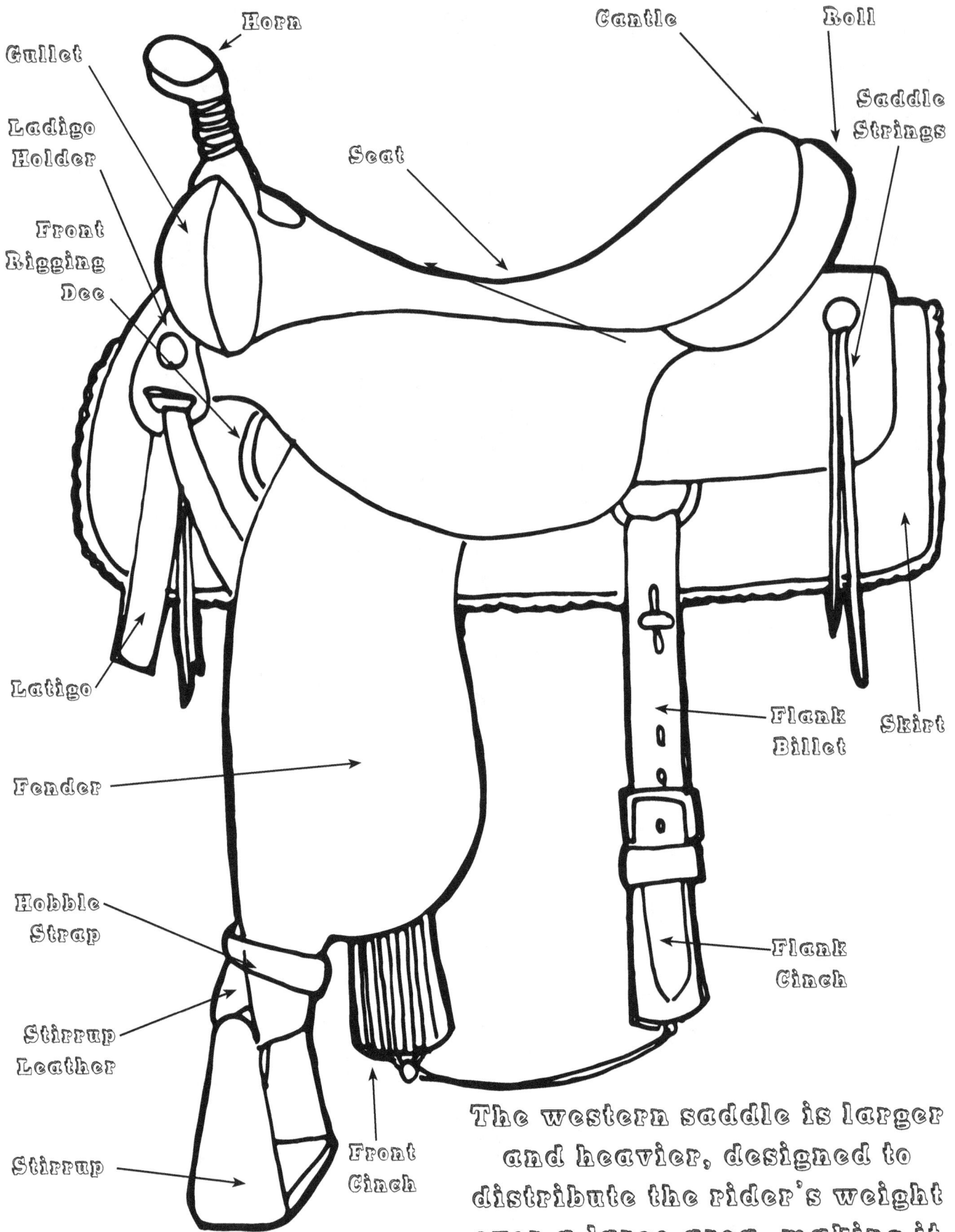

The western saddle is larger and heavier, designed to distribute the rider's weight over a large area, making it more comfortable.

Parts of a Western Saddle

Pommel

Seat

Knee
Roll

Cantle

Skirt

Panel

Flap

Leather

Girth

Iron

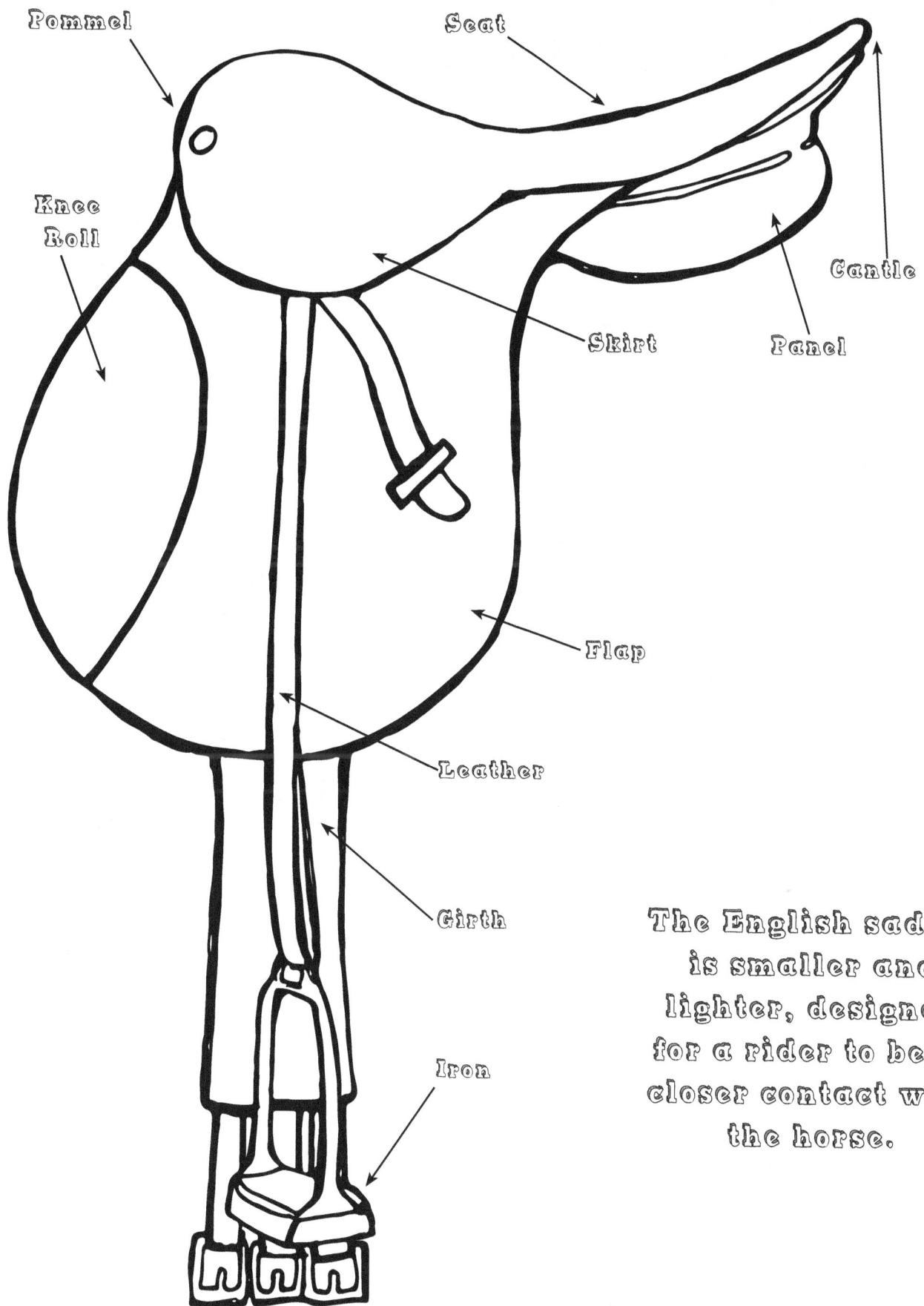

The English saddle
is smaller and
lighter, designed
for a rider to be in
closer contact with
the horse.

Parts of an English Saddle

Bitless Bridles

Mechanical Hackamore

Bitless bridles are often used to start young horses.

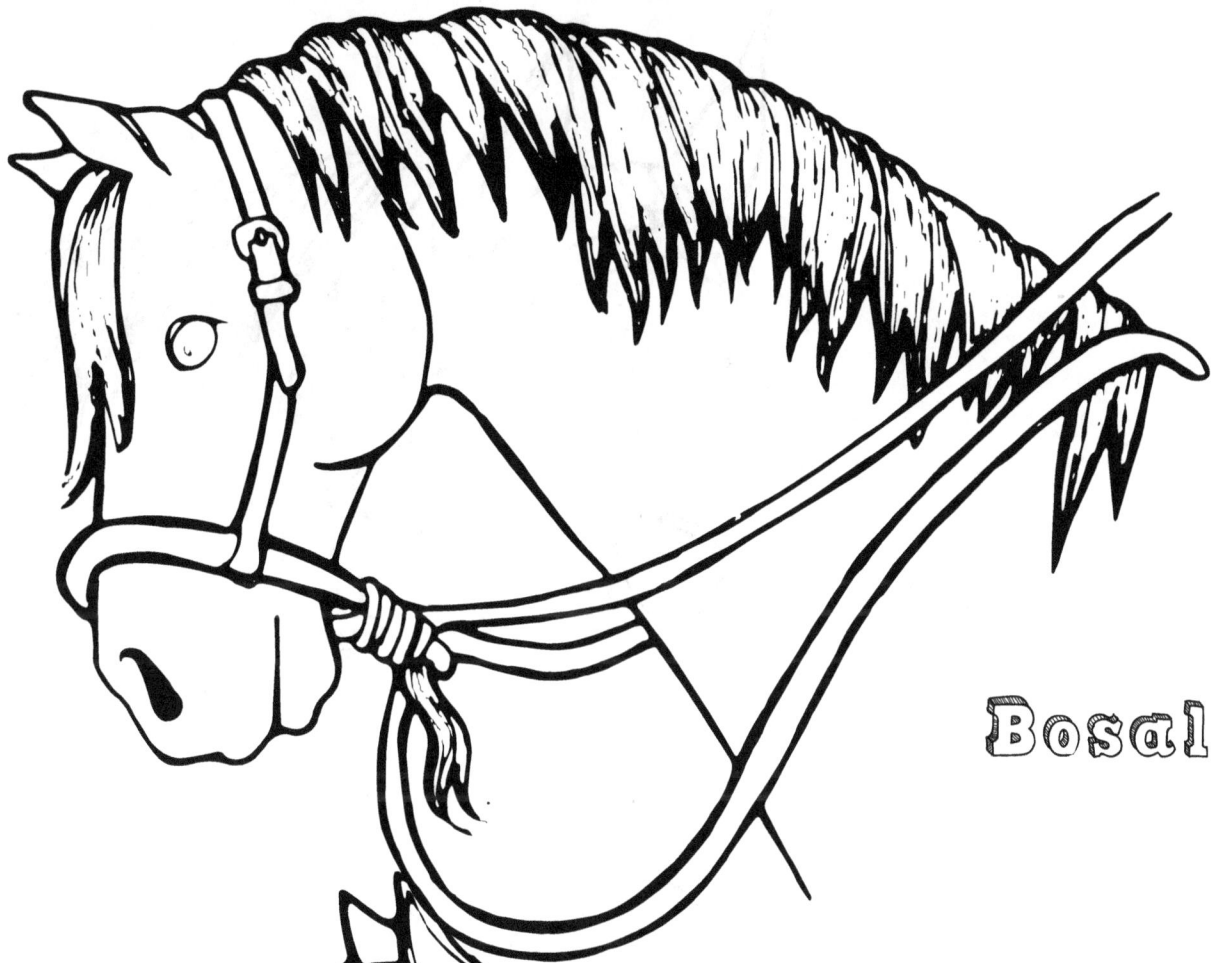

Bosal

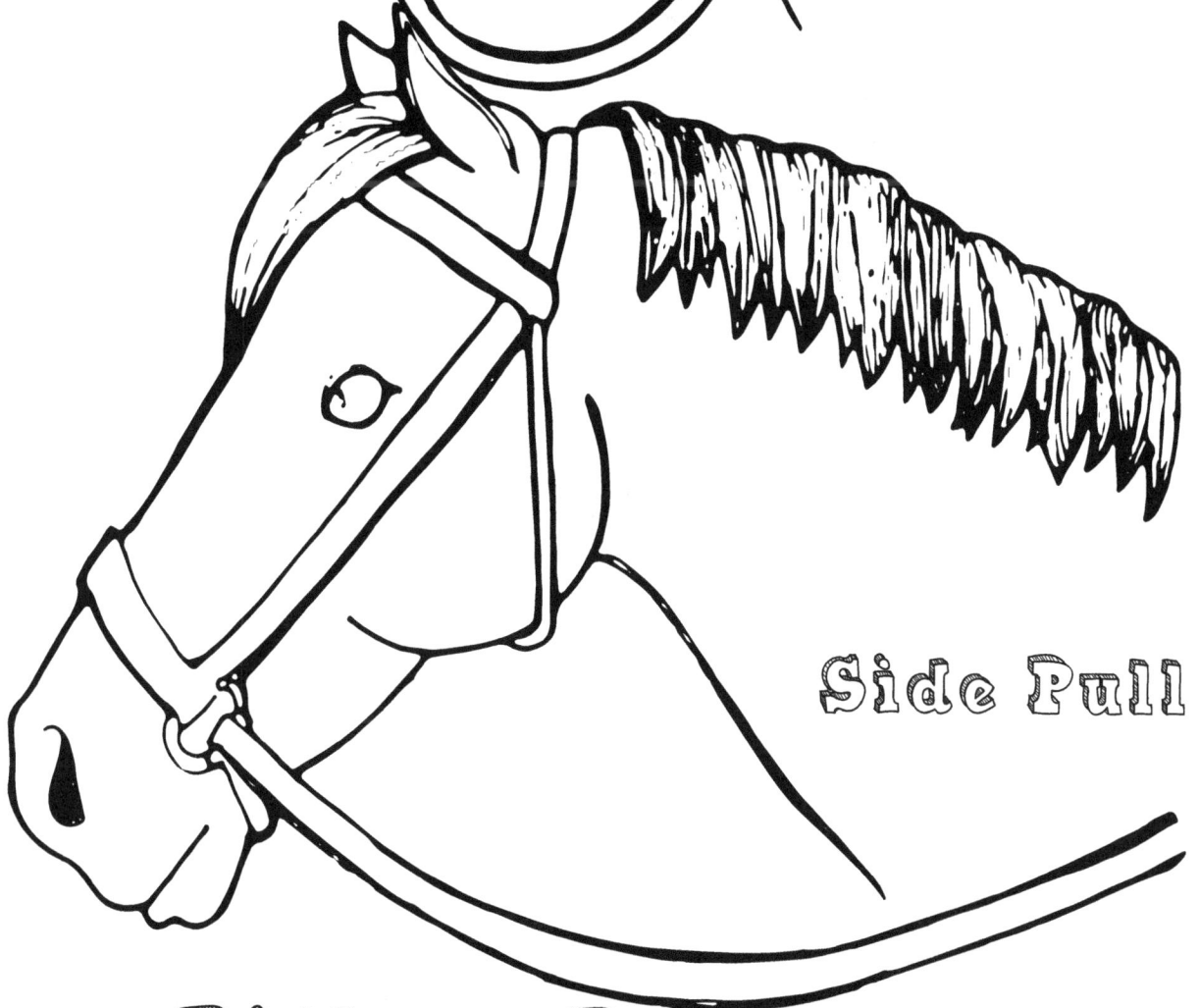

Side Pull

Bitless Bridles

Browband

Headstalls

One Ear

Vacquero
Crossover

Headstalls

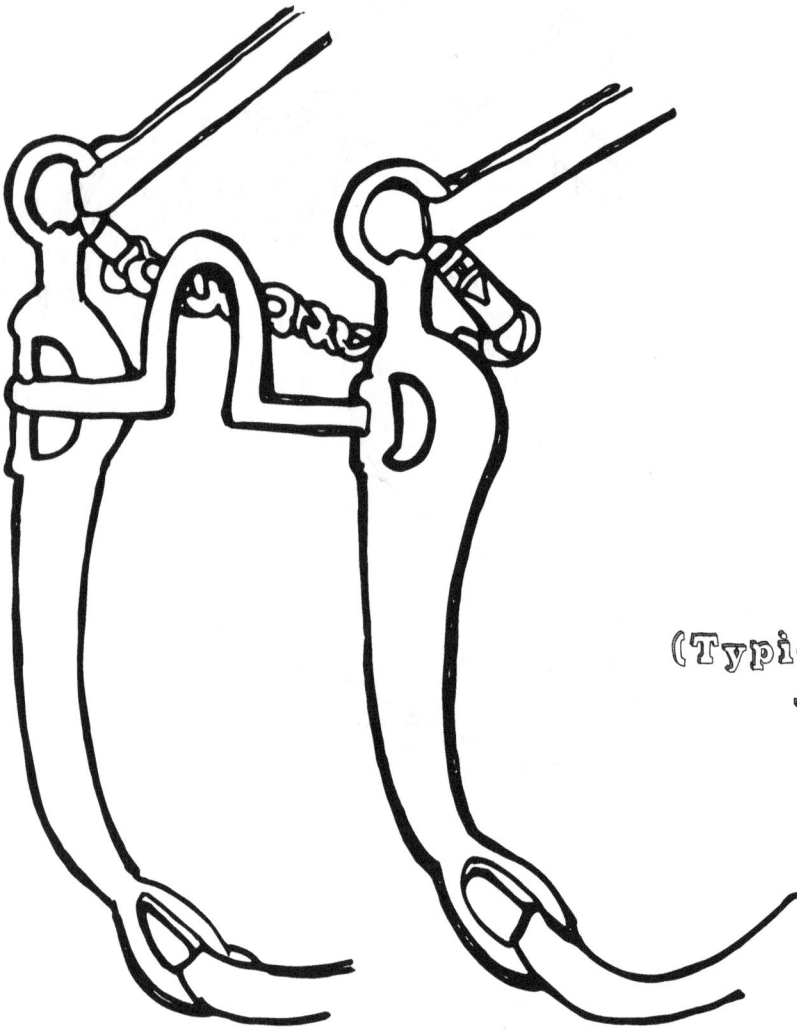

Curb
(Typical western bit with port)

Snaffle
(Often used to start a youngster)

(The more narrow the mouth piece, the more reactive it is.)

Types of Bits

Slobber Straps

Some Western riders use slobber straps, which were originally used close to the bit to avoid replacing the entire rein when it wears out. Today, slobber straps combined with heavy rope reins increase the amount of contact a rider has with the horse's mouth.

Romal Reins

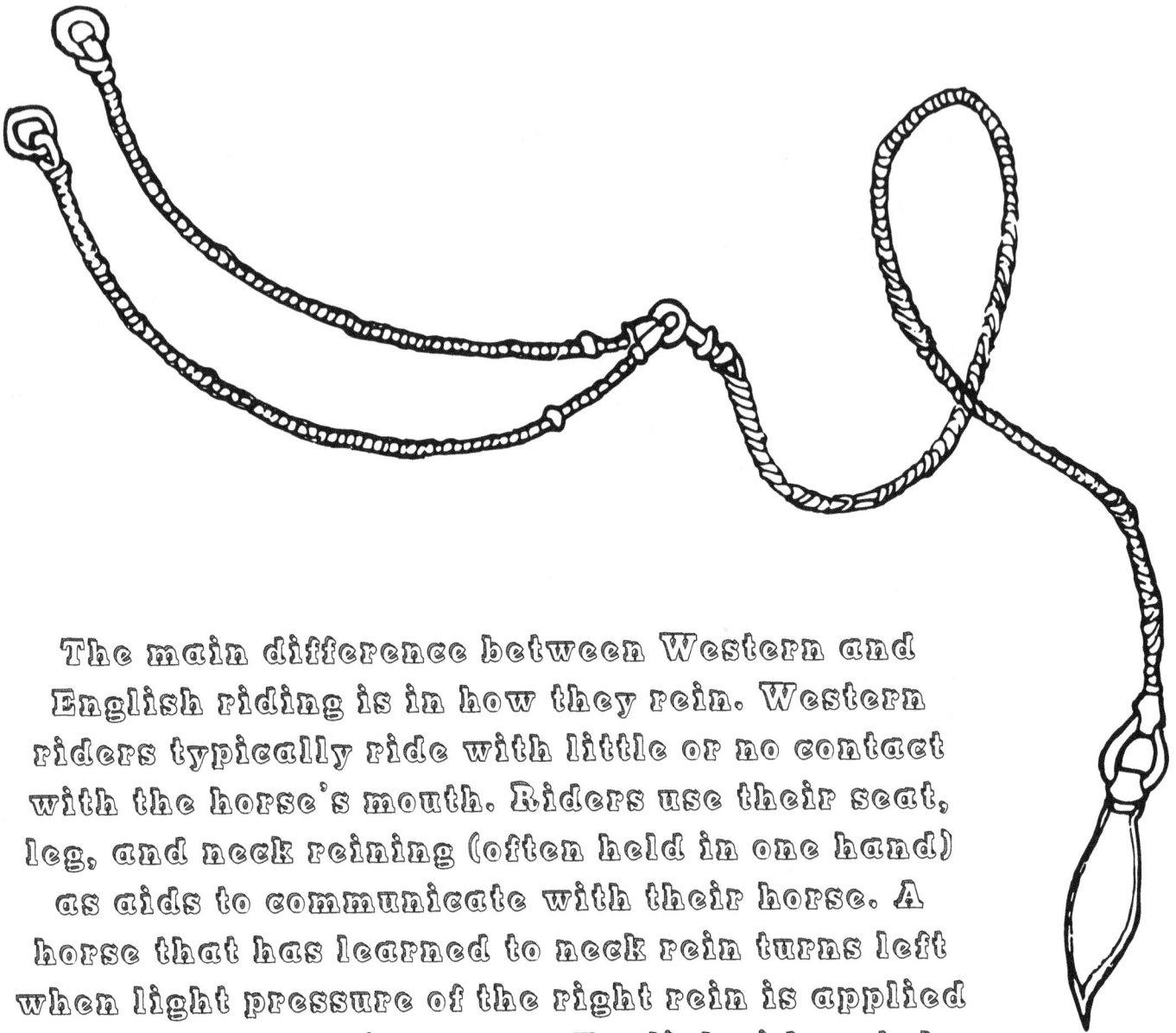

The main difference between Western and English riding is in how they rein. Western riders typically ride with little or no contact with the horse's mouth. Riders use their seat, leg, and neck reining (often held in one hand) as aids to communicate with their horse. A horse that has learned to neck rein turns left when light pressure of the right rein is applied to its neck, and vice versa. English riders take direct contact with the horse's mouth using the reins (held in both hands), seat, and leg as aids for speed and direction.

Romal reins, usually made of leather or rawhide, are connected to the bridle and used as a tool to assist in moving cattle.

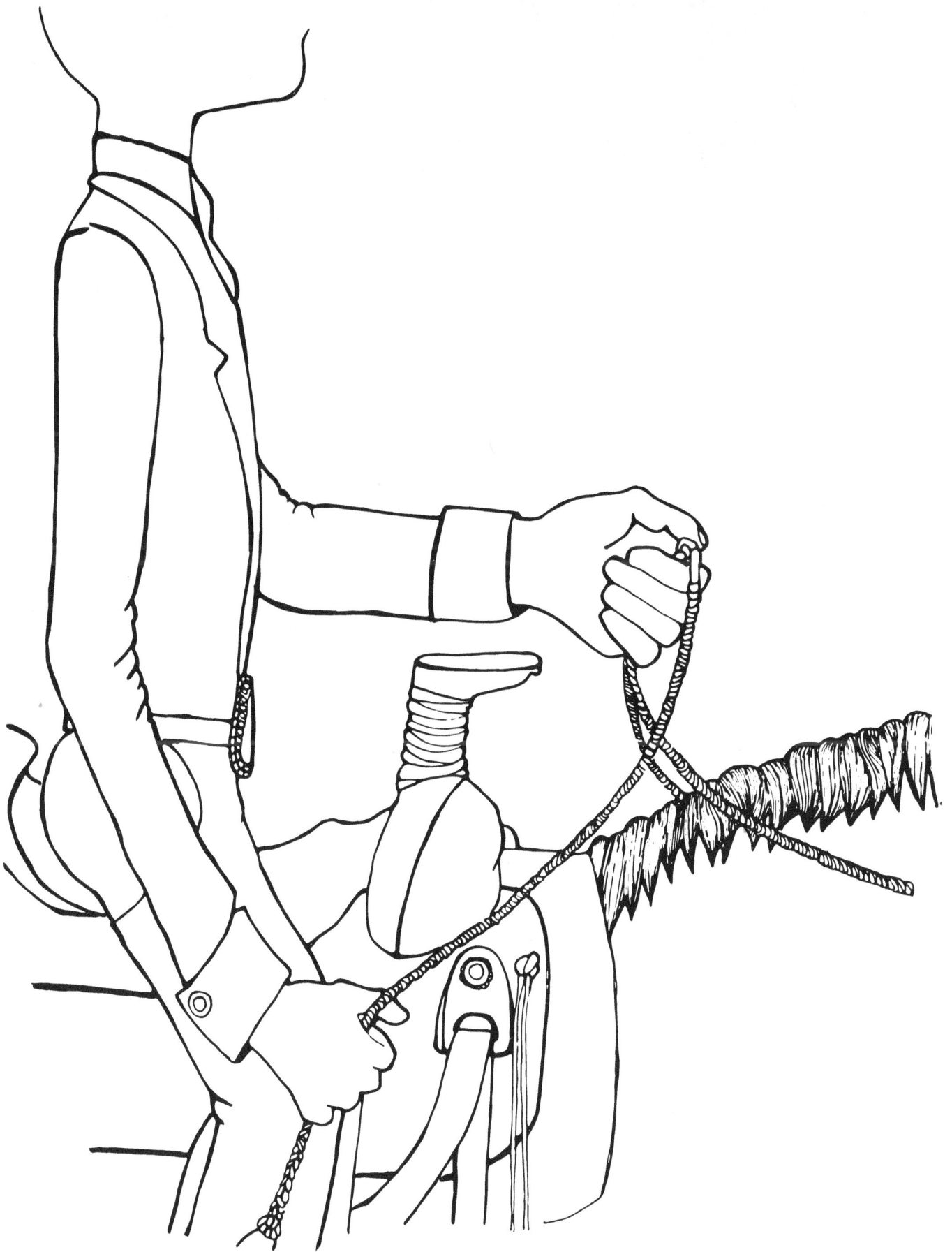

Proper Handset
with Romal Reins

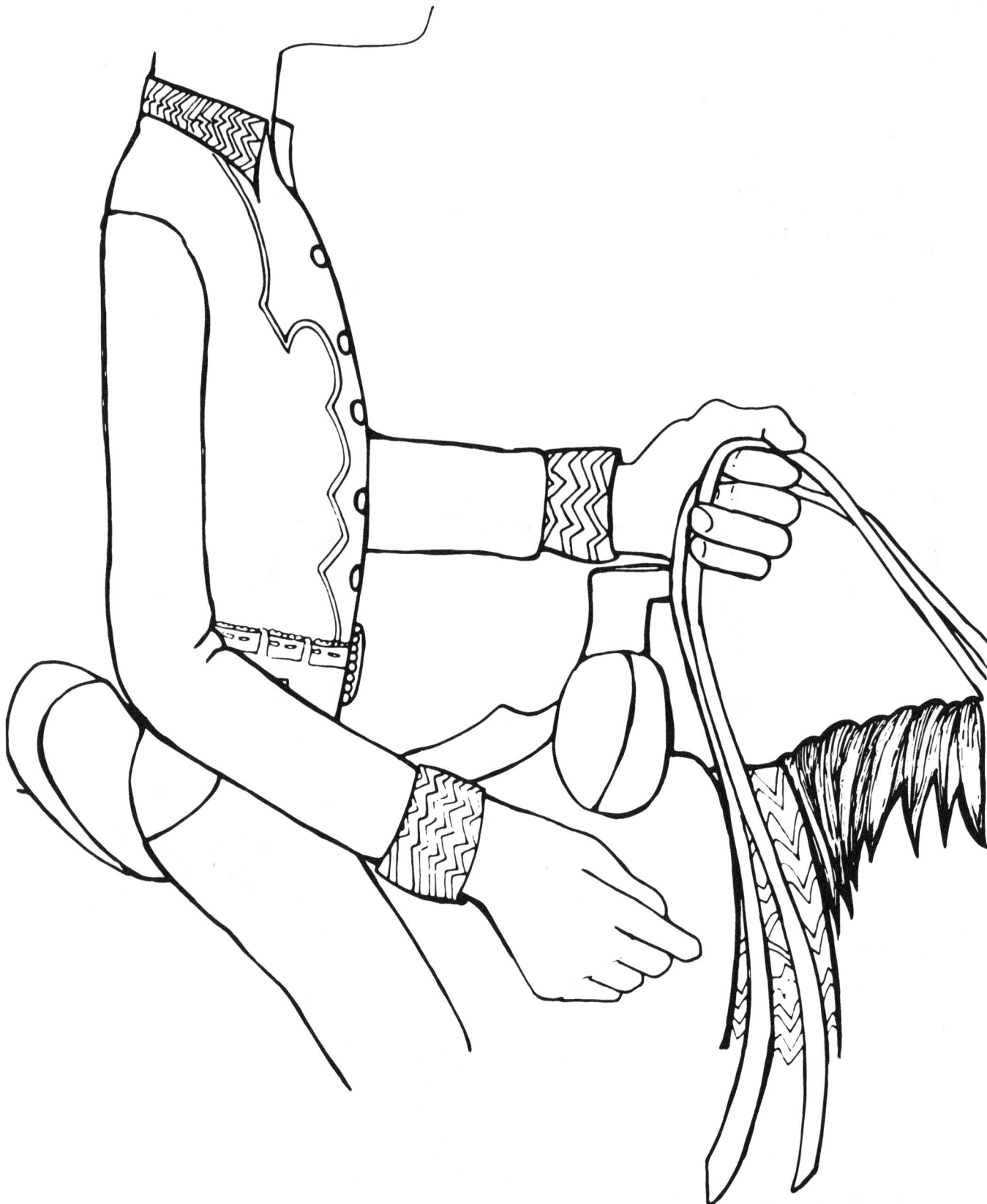

Western riders rode with one hand and neck reined because
they worked their ranches on horseback, using their other hand
to open and close gates and rope cattle.

Your index finger should be in between the reins, thumb on top,
with your other digits loosely supporting the reins.

How to Carry Split Reins

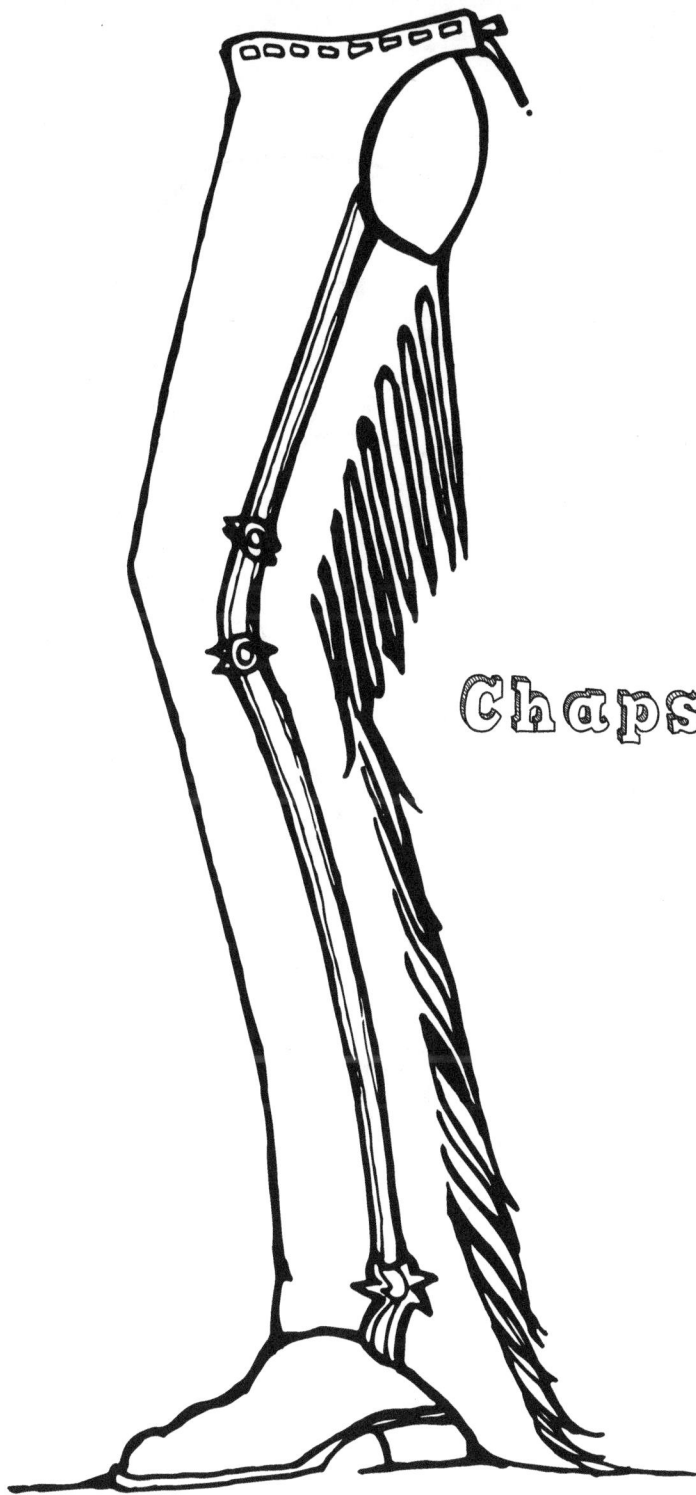

Chaps

Chinks

Western and English riders dress differently! You'll see pretty
standard Western attire throughout this book along with an
English rider sneaked in from time-to-time.

In hot climates, cowboys wear chinks, which are cooler and
allow for easier mounting and dismounting from their horse.

Chaps & Chinks

Western and English horses move a little differently, because they have slight differences in their gaits. (Gallop and walk are the same.) **Jog**

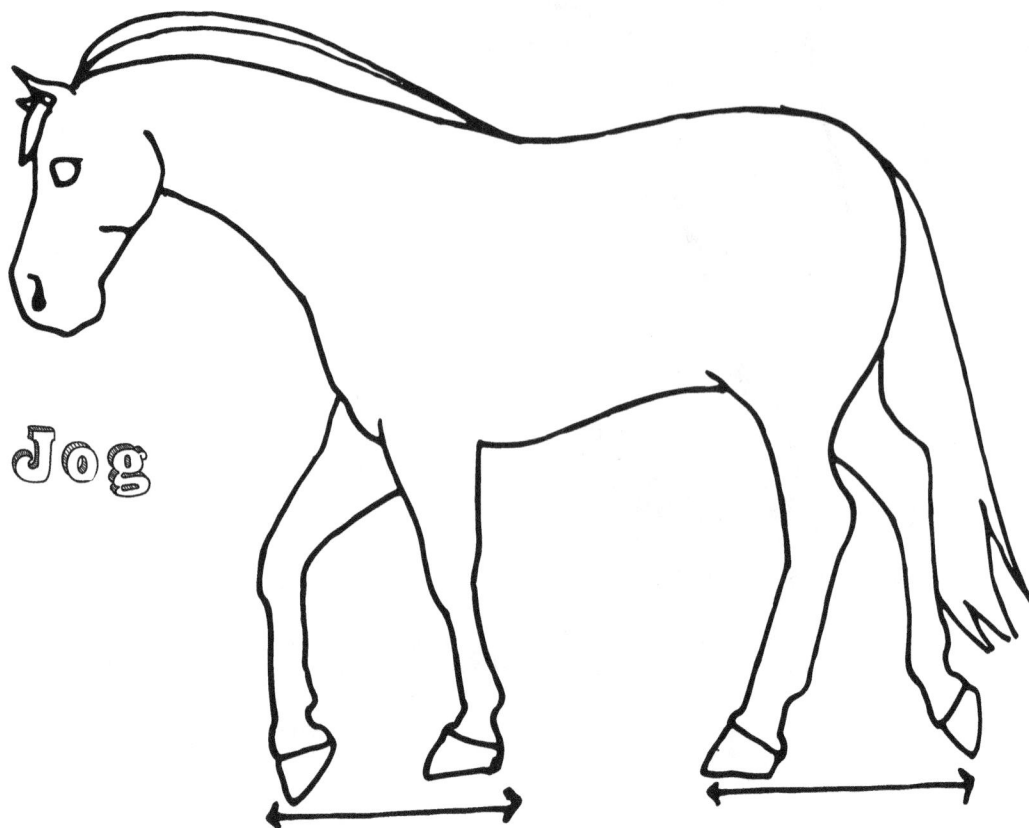

Trot

Western horses jog. English horses trot. Both are two-beat, diagonal gaits (the horse's right front and left rear hooves strike the ground at the same time). The only difference is the length of stride. The jog, while lively and ground-covering, is a shorter length, and therefore slower.

Jog vs. Trot

Lope

Canter

Western horses lope. English horses canter. Both are three-beat gaits. Like jog and trot, the only difference is the length of stride. The lope is a shorter length, and therefore slower.

Lope vs. Canter

Western Disciplines

Barrel Racing

Reining (sliding stop)

Showmanship and Halter

Trail Riding

FINISH
1,250 MILES (Really)

Endurance Rides

Roping

Western Pleasure

Western or English, some
horses are a little shy.

and some are scared of everything on the trails, while others couldn't care less what they're passing. Western or English, we wish "Happy Trails" to you!

Fun Fjord Fact: Typically Fjord manes are well-kept with the black stripe 1/4" taller. When left to grow out they tend to look a little like a hippie!

We're always working on new books!
Write to us (fcfwalter@gmail.com) with
your comments, ideas, or suggestions.

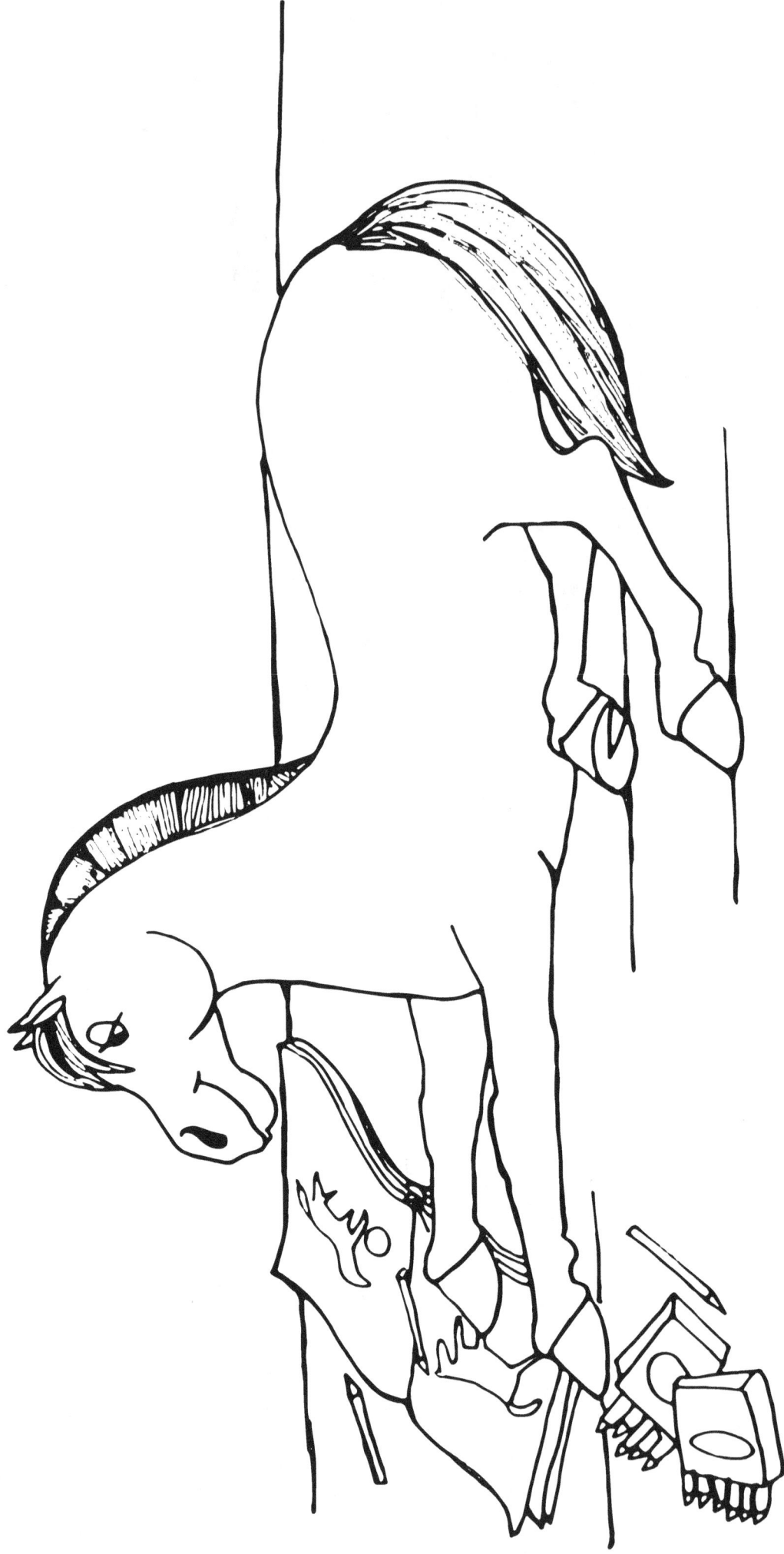

You might also like:

Color Your Way Into English Riding 1!

Francis Creek Fjords Coloring Books

Color Your Way Into
English Riding 1

By Patti Jo Walter and Pat Holland

Francis Creek Fjords Coloring Books

Color Your Way Into
English Riding 2

By Patti Jo Walter and Pat Holland

Color Your Way Into English Riding 2!

Francis Creek Fjords Coloring Books

Color Your Way Into
Horse Driving

By Patti Jo Walter and Pat Holland

Color Your Way Into Horse Driving!

Color Your Way Into A Horse for Christmas!

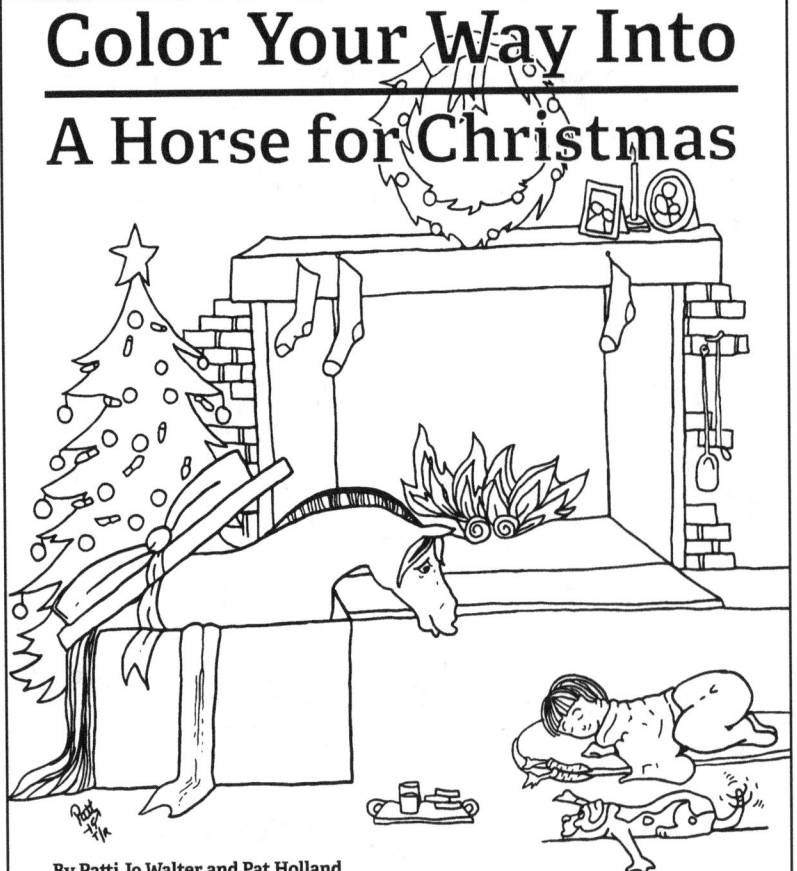

Francis Creek Fjords Coloring Books

Color Your Way Into
A Horse for Christmas

By Patti Jo Walter and Pat Holland

and ...
Color Your Way Into
Horseback Riding!
(includes English 1 & 2 and Western)

Francis Creek Fjords Coloring **Books**

Color Your Way Into
Horseback Riding

TEAM WHOA

FCF

By Patti Jo Walter and Pat Holland

www.ingramcontent.com/pod-product-compliance
Lightning Source LLC
Chambersburg PA
CBHW081252040426
42452CB00015B/2796